THE REGENCY GUIDE TO SEDUCTION

First published in 2025 by Welbeck Illustrated
An imprint of Headline Publishing Group Limited

Text by Sarah Herman
Illustrations © Louisa Cannell
Editor: Anna Martin
Design by Rebecca Hills

1

Cataloguing in Publication Data is available from the British Library

ISBN 978-1-0354-2982-0

Printed and bound in China

HEADLINE PUBLISHING GROUP LIMITED
An Hachette UK Company
Carmelite House
50 Victoria Embankment
London EC4Y 0DZ

The authorised representative in the EEA is Hachette Ireland,
8 Castlecourt Centre, Dublin 15, D15 XTP3, Ireland (email: info@hbgi.ie)

www.headline.co.uk
www.hachette.co.uk

THE REGENCY GUIDE TO SEDUCTION

LOVE ADVICE FOR MODERN HEROINES

LADY BENNET-DOWN

ILLUSTRATIONS BY LOUISA CANNELL

WELBECK

Contents

Dear beautiful, bewildered reader,

It is a truth universally acknowledged that the modern world of courtship can at times be compared to a steaming pile of horse excrement.

While you would most likely be excused for taking one sharp look at your current dating condition, shedding all decorum and crying out, 'Is this all there is?!' I urge you not to despair. Dramatics are very rarely alluring, except in the bedchamber. Instead, why not channel that energy into buckling up, bracing oneself, and stepping out once again.

Here I share my pearls of wisdom, gleaned from traversing the peaks and troughs of love's lumpy landscape like a Georgian member of the *Geordie Shore* cast. From first dates to final breaks, awkward dinners to dancefloor disasters, and PDA to MIA, let me give breath to some of the most commonly ruinous dilemmas contemporary daters face.

So set aside your cynicism, banish those bad-date memories, and prepare to heed my advice, because the dating game is not over, dear reader. In fact, it has only just begun.

Yours passionately and provocatively,

Lady Bennet-Down

I

THE MEET-CUTE

'EVERY MOMENT HAD ITS PLEASURES AND ITS HOPE.'

***SENSE AND SENSIBILITY*, JANE AUSTEN**

THE THRILL OF A FIRST IMPRESSION – ITS INTRIGUE, MYSTERY AND TANTALIZING POTENTIAL – LEAVES MANY OF US FLUSTERED AND FUMBLING. BUT FEAR NOT, DEAR READER. WITH A DEFT TOUCH AND A PINCH OF WIT, YOU MAY SET THE STAGE FOR AN UNFORGETTABLE BEGINNING, RICH IN PROMISE AND POSSIBILITY (AND HOPEFULLY NOT TOO MANY DICK PICS).

CENSORED

I MET SOMEONE AT THE SUPERMARKET – WE WERE BOTH BROWSING THE FRUIT AND VEG AND THERE WAS AN IMMEDIATE SPARK, BUT I FORGOT TO GET THEIR NUMBER. HOW DO I ARRANGE ANOTHER 'CHANCE' MEETING?

Dear melon-choly reader,

Behold the sweet serendipity of a fruitful meeting! Few things delight the heart so much as a well-timed rendezvous that owes all to Lady Luck. But the Lady can be fickle, so she might need a gentle nudge. With that in mind, get thee to the market post-haste on the same day the following week. Attend a trifle earlier, so you can position yourself by the ripest of fruits. Chance meetings, after all, always benefit from a modicum of planning.

If the apple of your eye shares your affections, it's likely you'll find them roaming the same stalls, perusing juicy peaches in the hopes of a second encounter. However, there is also a chance they might just be picking up some provisions for their next green smoothie. So do not pursue them too vehemently, as this might alarm their gentil sensibilities. Remember, the appearance of spontaneity is key – be sure to look the very picture of surprise.

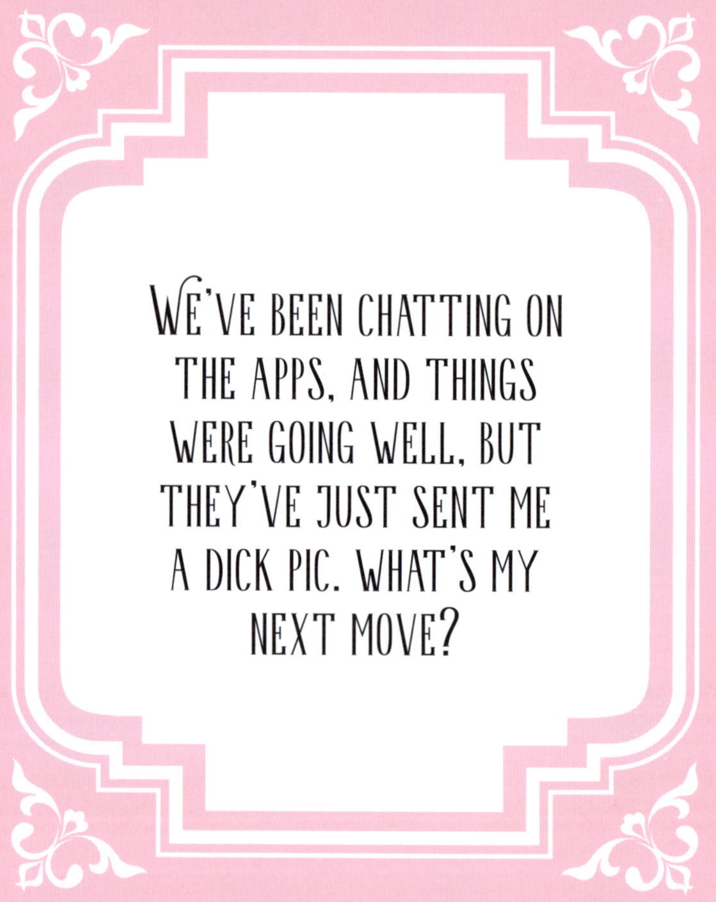

WE'VE BEEN CHATTING ON THE APPS, AND THINGS WERE GOING WELL, BUT THEY'VE JUST SENT ME A DICK PIC. WHAT'S MY NEXT MOVE?

Dear crimsoned reader,

First of all, allow yourself to feel shocked, because there's nothing like the audacious spectacle of an uninvited self-portrait. Modern courtship is rife with surprises, albeit some are less welcome than others. If a gentleman (or gentlewoman for that matter) elects to display their assets without proper invitation, consider this an indication of their character.

The proper response depends on your own sensibilities. Has this impromptu artwork left you thoroughly appalled and unimpressed? Perhaps a light quip or a sharp rebuke is in order. For example, 'Thank you for that kind reminder to pick up some baby carrots,' or 'Oh god! What happened to your pet rat?' Or how about a tactful silence – it might be all the response you need. It serves as a subtle reminder that courtship is a delicate dance best conducted with decorum.

If you would like to continue to converse, make it clear such advances are premature. And remember, genuine charm and good taste rarely require such bold displays. We are not peacocks, after all. If your messages fall on deaf ears, their character (and contents of their lunchbox) might be unworthy of your time altogether.

I MET SOMEONE CUTE AT A PARTY AND THEY'VE JUST MESSAGED ME. IS IT OK TO STALK THEM ONLINE BEFORE I RESPOND OR IS THAT AN INVASION OF THEIR PRIVACY?

Dear curious reader,

What can I say about the need for 'research' before romance? In days past, one would rely upon whispered reputations and the subtle inquiries of well-placed friends. Now a full dossier lies but a few taps away.

By all means, ensure they're not secretly wed or a cult leader. And do enjoy the lighter discoveries. Perhaps you share a love of avant-garde theatre. Or maybe they have an inordinate fondness for dressing their dachshund in tiny waistcoats. Such titbits offer delightful glimpses into their character, which may provide excellent fodder for future conversation.

Should you find yourself twenty posts deep in their ex-partner's wedding photos, it may be prudent to stop digging and let the mystery linger. After all, some secrets are best uncovered in person, one flirtation at a time!

'His company so sought after, that every body says he need not eat a single meal by himself if he does not chuse it; that he has more invitations than there are days in the week.'

Emma, Jane Austen

Lady Bennet-Down's Tips

- ## EMBRACE YOUR CHARM

  Worry not over every word; a suitor drawn to your natural wit will not be discouraged by lively conversation.

- ## SUBTLETY IS KEY

  Catch their eye with grace, for a mere glance or smile can prompt even the shyest admirer to step forward.

- ## MYSTERY IS YOUR GREATEST FRIEND

  No need to impress with ceaseless chatter; a few words and an attentive ear will leave them wanting more.

- ## LOVE IS A GAME OF 'CHANCE'

  Should fate need a gentle nudge, make it appear as happenstance.

- ## TAKE THE LEAP

  If correspondence lags, feel free to make the first move, for confidence is always fetching and you've got some serious flirting to do.

- ## ASSESS WITH CAUTION

  When arranging a first encounter (or simply writing flirtatious messages) look for signs of sincere interest, gentile conduct and a measured use of emojis.

II

THE INVITATION

'... YOU NEED NOT BE SO ALARMED ABOUT HIM. I DID INVITE HIM, YOU KNOW. I SENT HIM AWAY WITH SMILES.'

***PERSUASION*, JANE AUSTEN**

I do love
an iced ring

THE PATHWAY TO A PROPER INVITATION CAN BE FRAUGHT WITH UNCERTAINTY: IS YOUR DATE EAGER TO GET TO KNOW YOU OR JUST YOUR UNDERGARMENTS? DOES THIS CASUAL CERAMICS CLASS CARRY A DEEPER MEANING OR ARE THEY JUST REALLY INTO MAKING POTS? WHETHER SPARKING ROMANCE FROM FRIENDSHIP OR DELICATELY PURSUING A SECOND DATE, EACH INVITATION CARRIES WEIGHT, CHARM AND JUST A TOUCH OF PERIL (ESPECIALLY IF THEY WANT TO GO ICE SKATING). PROCEED WITH BOTH GRACE AND TENACITY, DEAR READER, FOR COURTSHIP FAVOURS THE BOLD.

I'VE BEEN TEXTING SOMEONE FOR WEEKS AND THEY FINALLY INVITED ME TO GO FOR COFFEE. HOW CAN I BE SURE IT'S A DATE, RATHER THAN A CASUAL FRIEND MEET-UP OR, WORSE, A NETWORKING OPPORTUNITY?

Dear decaffeinated reader,

An invitation to society's finest coffee house can leave even the most besotted beau out of sorts. Is it a subtle ruse – a suggestion of friendship when the bright lights of romance are just around the corner? Or simply an opportune moment to discuss business affairs over the latest roast rather than affairs of the heart?

As you prepare for the outing, consider some of the fundamental signs. Did the invitation include a cheeky emoji and did your acquaintance enquire about your favourite brew? Or did their message mention marketing spend or sales strategies? If it's the latter (or should that be latte), it's unlikely there's a romantic finger sandwich in your future.

And what about the locale? Did they pick somewhere loud and bustling to meet or an intimate nook ideal for cosying up over caffeine? While you don't want to find yourself in a platonic pitfall, be bold. Even a 'friend date' may hold hidden delights (and I'm not just talking about the cinnamon buns) if approached with an open heart.

'You take delight in vexing me. You have no compassion for my poor nerves!'

Pride and Prejudice, Jane Austen

Lady Bennet-Down's Tips

- ## STRIKE THE PERFECT BALANCE

  Be neither too keen nor too aloof. Too much enthusiasm can reek of desperation, while silence may suggest your attention is engaged elsewhere.

- ## PICK THE PERFECT SETTING

  Opt for a locale that suits your intentions – whether a charming café, a stimulating art gallery, or the nearest Nando's (no judgement).

- ## ADD A TOUCH OF MYSTERY

  Instead of spelling out every detail, leave some room for intrigue. A hint of uncertainty can heighten anticipation and encourage curiosity.

- ## LIGHTEN UP

  An invitation should be far from solemn. A playful suggestion or aubergine emoji is often more appealing and keeps things flirtatious without piling on the pressure.

- ## RESPECT THEIR COMFORT LEVELS

  Not everyone responds swiftly to invitations. If they hesitate, grant them a reasonable amount of time to warm to the idea – or politely bid you farewell.

- ## LET THE INVITATION SPEAK FOR ITSELF

  Avoid grand gestures, elaborate explanations or rambling voice notes. A simple, unambiguous invite shows confidence and allows room for genuine connection.

'When he was present she had no eyes for any one else. Every thing he did, was right. Every thing he said, was clever.'

Sense and Sensibility, Jane Austen

III

THE FIRST DATE

'OH, SHE IS THE MOST BEAUTIFUL CREATURE I EVER BEHELD!'

***PRIDE AND PREJUDICE*, JANE AUSTEN**

THE FINER POINTS HAVE BEEN AGREED, THE CANDLES ARE LIT AND IT'S FINALLY TIME TO EMBARK ON YOUR MAIDEN VOYAGE TOGETHER. THERE IS NOTHING QUITE LIKE A FIRST DATE: BUTTERFLIES IN YOUR STOMACH, STOLEN GLANCES, WONDERING IF THEIR HAND INTENTIONALLY BRUSHED AGAINST YOUR OWN OR WERE THEY JUST REACHING FOR THE KETCHUP?

I AM HERE TO HELP YOU HANDLE THOSE FIRST-DATE JITTERS, SET THE WHEELS IN MOTION FOR FUTURE DALLIANCES AND DEFEND YOUR HEART AGAINST ANY ATTACK THIS EARLY IN THE DATING GAME.

FANS AT THE READY ...

WE MET UP FOR THE FIRST TIME AND THEY SPENT HALF THE DATE ON THEIR PHONE, CHECKING NOTIFICATIONS AND SCROLLING. IS THAT A RED FLAG?

Dear indignant reader,

One cannot deny the insatiable preoccupation many people have with their electronic devices is the height of impropriety. How dare this potential suitor disregard all politeness by focusing their attentions on the distractions of virtual society, when the brightest light of them all is sitting across from them?

This persistent glow must not diminish yours, but be sure to give them a second chance to set the record straight – perhaps there was a family emergency or work problem they couldn't ignore. The next time you meet, if this distraction persists, be sure to voice your discontent with a light touch. Something like, 'Am I in competition with the group chat?'

Hopefully, they will recognize the error of their ways and pocket their phone for the remainder of the evening. If not, it's fair to say your wit and beauty are no match for the latest football scores or the enticement of other potential matches. Unsheathe your phone and book an Uber.

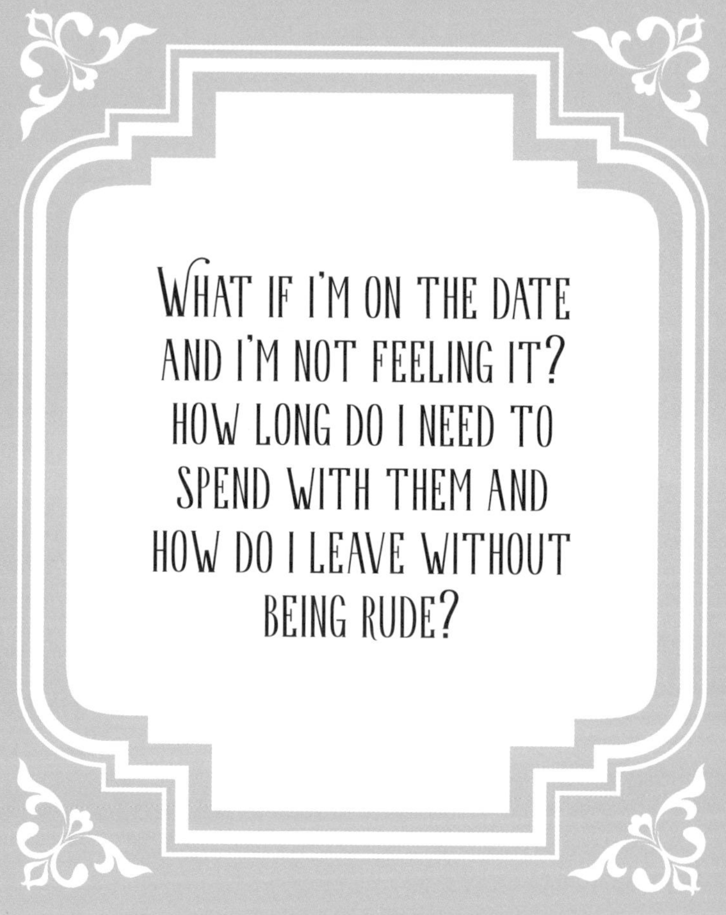
WHAT IF I'M ON THE DATE
AND I'M NOT FEELING IT?
HOW LONG DO I NEED TO
SPEND WITH THEM AND
HOW DO I LEAVE WITHOUT
BEING RUDE?

Dear considerate reader,

Alas, sometimes even the most promising of courtships can come up short. Perhaps they've made an off-colour joke you can't ignore. Or they've droned on about their collection of antique china dolls. Maybe you've just experienced the 'ick' and you cannot find the cause.

It's prudent to devise an exit strategy that is both respectful and courteous (unless your companion has been neither of these things, in which case, all bets are off). Feeling sheepish? Politely impart that you have had a lovely time but prior engagements mean your attention is required elsewhere – or receive an 'important call' from a friend at just the right moment.

If you're partial to a more truthful approach, the floor is yours. Simply express that while you appreciated their company, you feel the connection is not giving romance vibes. With that said, don't underestimate the impact of first-date nerves. Giving a jittery suitor the benefit of the doubt, could unearth unexpected treasures. As their confidence builds, they may feel more relaxed and show parts of themselves previously hidden (hopefully not those parts – at least until you've consented and you're in a private setting).

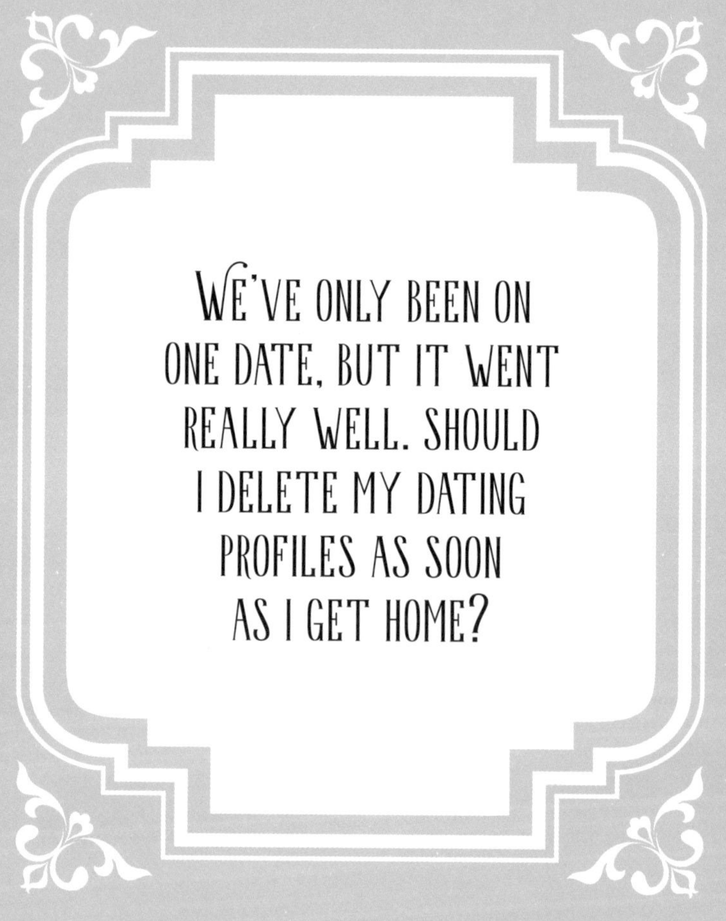
WE'VE ONLY BEEN ON
ONE DATE, BUT IT WENT
REALLY WELL. SHOULD
I DELETE MY DATING
PROFILES AS SOON
AS I GET HOME?

Dear socially conscious reader,

Was it not Shakespeare's Romeo who decried: 'Did my heart love till now? Forswear it, sight! / For I ne'er saw true beauty till this night' mere moments after catching sight of fair Juliet? In light of Romeo's haste and swift demise, I fear your willingness to curtail the possibility of other alliances might be premature.

Deleting your profiles sends a signal of seriousness and intention – a sign that you are all-in on this single connection. But it might have the adverse effect on your suitor, should they find out and feel you're coming on too strong. Steady yourself – it's not time to pick out the wedding list just yet! With uncertainty still lingering, keeping your options open may be the most prudent course – whether you choose to engage with new connections or not.

Lady Bennet-Down's Tips

✦ DRESS TO DAZZLE, BUT FOR YOURSELF FIRST

Choose an ensemble that bolsters your confidence, rather than constricts your lung capacity, for nothing captivates more than self-assurance.

✦ TEMPER YOUR PREJUDICE

Don't be drawn into judgement too quickly. The time it takes to sip one sherry is not nearly enough to fully know a person or their suitability as a partner.

✦ GET THE ATTENTION YOU DESERVE

If your date spends half the time fiddling with their devices, say something. A playful quip might get things back on track.

✦ HAVE AN EXIT STRATEGY

Not every first date kindles the fires of romance. A kind word and a parting smile will suffice if your loins aren't burning (they're probably thinking the exact same thing).

✦ DON'T RUSH IN

Depositing all one's metaphorical eggs into a single partially studied basket is foolish. Hold your course before cutting off all other prospects and give this ember the chance to ignite.

✦ STAY CURIOUS

Enter each first date with the thrill of discovery but no strict agenda. Sometimes, true affection (and social awareness) takes time to surface.

IV

THE BALL

'TO BE FOND OF DANCING WAS A CERTAIN STEP TOWARDS FALLING IN LOVE.'

***PRIDE AND PREJUDICE*, JANE AUSTEN**

WHAT A DELIGHT FOR THE SENSES! THIS IS WHERE YOU SEE YOUR HEART'S DESIRE OUT IN THE WILD, BUMPING, GRINDING AND MINGLING WITH THEIR NEAREST AND DEAREST. YOU'LL EXPERIENCE GREATER INSIGHT AND APPRECIATION FOR WHO THEY ARE AND HOW THEY MOVE, SOCIALLY AND CHOREOGRAPHICALLY. SO DON YOUR FINEST ATTIRE, SLIP INTO THOSE DANCING SHOES, AND LET'S GO TO THE BALL!

I'M ABOUT TO MEET THEIR BESTIES FOR THE FIRST TIME AT A PARTY. HOW CAN I MAKE A GOOD IMPRESSION WITHOUT COMING ACROSS TOO EAGER?

Dear judicious reader,

Meeting your beloved's companions is no small undertaking. A party can feel like a salon of scrutiny - their friends the lions and you the unwitting antelope. Yet let me assure you, a calm countenance and a kind smile will earn you more favour than any show of enthusiasm ever could.

Aim to be engaging, but not overly familiar. A few thoughtful inquiries about their profession ('What is it that you do?'), their estate ('Do you live in London too?'), and their persuasion ('Cronuts or cruffins?') will endear you to them and help the conversation flow naturally. Should you find yourself in a large group, resist the urge to seek approval with a 'performance' of any kind. And whatever you do, for the love of all that is decent, do not belt out the entire soundtrack to *My Fair Lady* in your 'best' Cockney accent.

Just be your usual charming self and allow your wit and wisdom to shine in small doses. A well-placed compliment or genuine chuckle will win over the hardest hearts, without sacrificing a jot of dignity.

Cronuts or Cruffins?

I'M NOT MUCH OF A DANCER, BUT MY DATE LOVES TO BE ON THE DANCE FLOOR. HOW CAN I JOIN IN WITHOUT FEELING OUT OF PLACE?

Dear uncoordinated reader,

We cannot all be the jewel of the assembly, gliding gracefully across the ballroom like Beyoncé. If the dance floor is their domain, then consider yourself an honoured guest!

Fear not your two left feet. Instead, hone the skill of cheerful participation. Step lightly, sway gently and remember that if Strictly has taught us anything it's that enthusiasm can triumph over elegance. Allow your partner to lead, and they shall find delight in your willingness to join them in their joy.

Remember, being mediocre at dancing doesn't mean you won't make a top-tier partner in life – showing up with a smile and a sparkle in your eye will keep you in their good graces, regardless of your rhythm. You might stomp on the dancefloor, but you won't stomp all over their heart, and that's what really matters.

When we were dancing at the club, my date seemed more interested in grinding up against others than me. What's that all about?

Dear abandoned reader,

Your wariness is warranted, for it is one thing to enjoy the company (and buttocks) of others and quite another to make one's companion feel secondary by slut-dropping your way around the dance floor. The ballroom is a place of freedom and gaiety, yes, but it should also be an opportunity to bond and bring you closer as a couple.

If your partner's attentions were dispersed to the extent that you felt forgotten, this merits a gentle probe into their intentions.

Upon your next meeting, you might mention, with a smile, how you missed their company. Then observe their response. If they are quick to reassure and adjust, all is well. They'll probably prioritize you next time you step out for a quadrille (or mosh pit). But if they deflect or dismiss, it may signal a lack of consideration that could extend beyond the dance floor. Remember, a worthy partner makes you – and your booty – feel cherished in all company.

FRIEND
ZONED

'I only came for the sake of dancing with *you*.'

Northanger Abbey, Jane Austen

Lady Bennet-Down's Tips

ENTER WITH GRACE, NOT GRANDEUR

Make a splash if you so desire, but a quiet, confident entrance often speaks louder than gold, glitter or uncovered flesh.

MIND THE COMPANY YOU KEEP

When meeting your suitor's friends, be charming yet modest. Show interest without grandstanding or commandeering the conversation.

DANCE LIKE NO ONE'S WATCHING (EXCEPT YOUR PARTNER)

If dancing isn't your strength, remember: enthusiasm (and a shot of tequila) goes a long way.

ATTEND TO YOUR PARTNER

At social gatherings, let your beau feel free to shimmy solo, but don't neglect them. A graceful balance of trust and attention is key to a good night.

HANDLE TITLES WITH TACT

If introduced ambiguously, consider it a slip, not a slight. A gentle nudge afterwards will allow your suitor the chance to clarify without confrontation.

OBSERVE DANCE-FLOOR DIPLOMACY

If your partner's attention or hands wander to others, take note. Light-heartedly express your desire for more time together and assess their response.

V

The Dinner

'I SHOULD LIKE TO DINE WITH HIM;
I DARE SAY HE GIVES FAMOUS DINNERS.'

***Northanger Abbey*, Jane Austen**

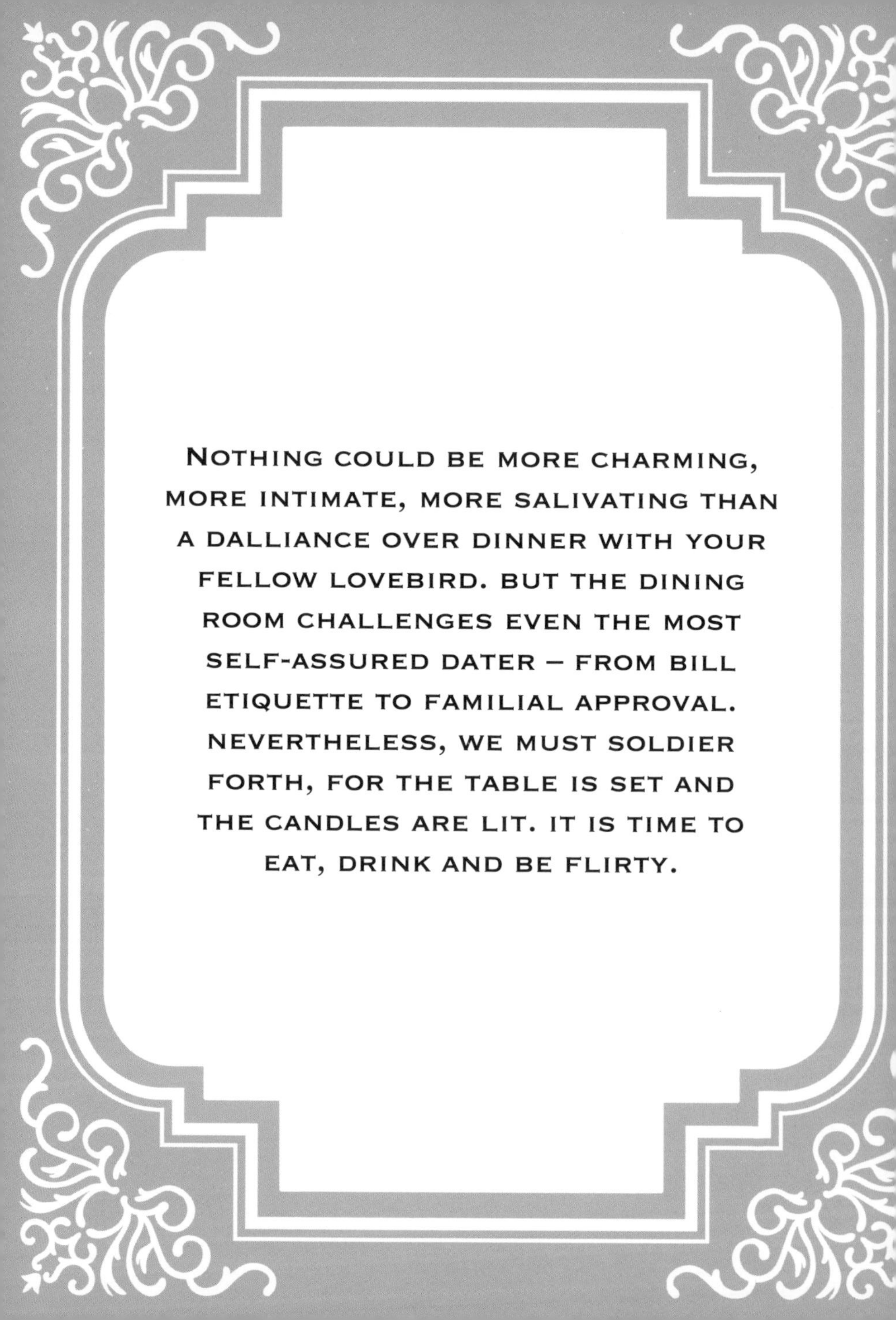

NOTHING COULD BE MORE CHARMING, MORE INTIMATE, MORE SALIVATING THAN A DALLIANCE OVER DINNER WITH YOUR FELLOW LOVEBIRD. BUT THE DINING ROOM CHALLENGES EVEN THE MOST SELF-ASSURED DATER – FROM BILL ETIQUETTE TO FAMILIAL APPROVAL. NEVERTHELESS, WE MUST SOLDIER FORTH, FOR THE TABLE IS SET AND THE CANDLES ARE LIT. IT IS TIME TO EAT, DRINK AND BE FLIRTY.

THEY ORDERED FOOD FOR BOTH OF US WITHOUT ASKING ME FIRST. SHOULD I SAY SOMETHING OR LET IT SLIDE?

Dear bemused reader,

It appears your date has assumed a rather forward approach! While some may view this as a charming display of initiative, others may feel their preferences (allergies and intolerances) have been callously disregarded. If you are inclined to address it, a light and playful approach is best. When the food arrives, you might smile and say, 'How adventurous! Though I'd love to choose my own dish next time' or, 'It would never occur to me to try the steak medium-rare!'

This cue, subtle or otherwise, should gently communicate your predilection without causing offense. If they take the hint and grab you a menu, all is well; if they don't, you may have uncovered an inclination to lead the dance without your involvement. In that case, consider if their captaincy aligns with your tastes – both over entrées and in life. Will they always insist on sourdough instead of olives? Will they never order dessert because their PT will be mad? And, worse, will they deny your desires beyond the dinner table?

We both reached for the bill at the same time, and now it's awkward. Should I insist on paying or let them take care of it?

Dear courteous reader,

The awkward dance of settling up is as old as time! Should you both extend your hand for the bill, a delicate rather than bullish approach is best. Politely say, 'Allow me,' and observe their response. If they truly wish to pay, gracefully accept their offer, as it may be an act of gallantry or habit on their part (or they might have a 2 for 1 voucher). However, should they hesitate, you might insist on treating them. Be sure to include a brief aside that they can get the next one. This affords the further pleasure of inferring another date is imminent.

Remember, sharing the cost of an evening is a mark of mutual respect and modern sensibility (as well as a necessity in most quarters). Should they accept your offer, let it be done with no further ado; and if they insist on treating you, a simple, 'thank you' will bring an elegant close to the matter. Whatever the outcome, the company enjoyed is, as ever, the truest currency of the evening.

Bill

Make mine
a foot long

I HAVE A BIG APPETITE, BUT I DON'T WANT THEM TO THINK I'M GREEDY. CAN I ORDER ALL THAT MY HEART DESIRES?

Dear bountiful reader,

In matters of the stomach, as with matters of the heart, it's not unusual for one to become blinded by abundance. Fortuitously, whilst a wandering eye for alternative suitors might sour any existing attachments, a penchant for pastry shouldn't be cause for alarm.

In fact, quite the opposite. It is customary in today's food-fascinated culture to indulge with some degree of regularity, whether you're sipping Bellinis over brunch, stomping across town to check out a new food truck or curating a charcuterie board to rival Instagram's finest artistes.

If they're not keen for seconds or only order a main course (while you add sides, a starter and dessert), they might still be worth keeping on the specials board. Just because you don't share the same appetite at the dinner table, it doesn't mean your hunger for each other is any less ravenous. But if they cast aspersions on your appetite, take your order to go. The bounteous buffet that is your life is not open to just anyone, and certainly not to them.

‘I BELIEVE, IN MANY MEN, ESPECIALLY SINGLE MEN, SUCH AN INCLINATION – SUCH A PASSION FOR DINING OUT – A DINNER ENGAGEMENT IS SO HIGH IN THE CLASS OF THEIR PLEASURES, THEIR EMPLOYMENTS, THEIR DIGNITIES, ALMOST THEIR DUTIES, THAT ANY THING GIVES WAY TO IT.’

EMMA, JANE AUSTEN

Lady Bennet-Down's Tips

LET YOUR PREFERENCES SHINE

Allowing someone to order for you may make you agreeable, but sharing the menu is the foundation of shared respect.

GRACE UNDER SCRUTINY

When meeting provocative friends or parents, charm, poise and a brisk deflection speak louder than over-rehearsed answers. Be gracious, not defensive.

CONFIDENCE OVER CLARET

If your enjoyment of the evening doesn't rely on a glass of wine, be proud of your sparkling water. Authenticity is far more intoxicating.

THE BILL IS NOT A BATTLEFIELD

When it comes to settling up, generosity and compromise go hand in hand. Keep the exchange light and thoughtful, and always offer to pay your way.

APPETITE IS ATTRACTIVE

One's love for a hearty meal (or not) is no bearing on good character. Don't deny yourself life's pleasure or deny your date getting to know the real you.

BEWARE THE MENU MISMATCH

If their tastes exceed your budget, be vigilant and seek out venues that satisfy both their cravings and your purse.

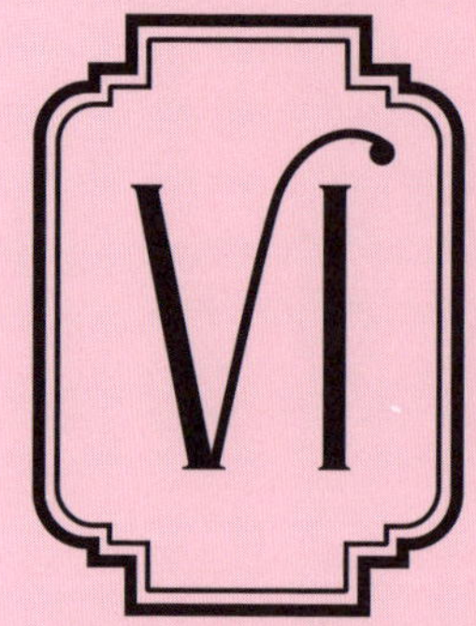
VI

DO NOT
DISTURB

The Sex

'MY FEELINGS WILL NOT BE REPRESSED. YOU MUST ALLOW ME TO TELL YOU HOW ARDENTLY I ADMIRE AND LOVE YOU.'

***Pride and Prejudice*, Jane Austen**

Salutations! You have survived the perilous social slalom of modern dating and crash-banged (quite literally) here, dear reader, into the main event. Sex is the erotic denouement to all that flirting and the humping off point for whatever comes next (hopefully you).

Sexual escapades, appetites and idiosyncrasies can cause the rise or fall of new love, so they're best approached with consideration (or, at the very least, suitable protection). Whether you're a lascivious libertine with loose morals and undergarments or a naïve novice tentatively taking your first steps into carnal waters, be sure to feel your way through my advice, one sensual stroke at a time.

WE GOT CARRIED AWAY COMING HOME FROM A DATE. IS IT OK TO HAVE SEX IN PUBLIC?

Dear breathless reader,

Ah, the thrill of passion, so intoxicating that even the confines of a cab cannot deter its course. While your fervour is certainly to be admired, one must consider the propriety (and even legality) of such an impromptu rendezvous. A carriage ride may indeed feel like an intimate affair, but please spare a thought for your driver. Don't lose sight of the fact you're in a public place – probably not the ideal setting for such private matters, however frisky you might be feeling.

Sometimes putting pause on bubbling passions can heighten the excitement of what will happen when you finally reach your destination. And if the thrill of a public place is the only thing to get your heart racing, I implore you to reconsider the locale. Perhaps a deserted beach, quiet park or the back of your own car outside a supermarket might be a more suitable setting.

I'M WORRIED I DON'T HAVE THE BODY OF AN INSTAGRAM INFLUENCER AND THEY'LL BE TURNED OFF WHEN WE GET NAKED! EEK, HELP.

Dear self-conscious reader,

Firstly, let me offer a most liberating truth: what matters most is not one's shape or form, but the confidence with which you carry it. And in the words of the most exquisite of sages, Lady RuPaul, 'If you can't love yourself, how in the hell are you gonna love somebody else?'

Alas, the perils of comparison are something everyone is sadly too familiar with and must work hard to overcome, particularly at this pivotal point where one is preparing to launch into the sea of sexual escapades.

Your companion, if they are worthy of such an eyeful, is interested not in mere facades, but in the beauty of your soul and the tenderness of your touch – they may think your body is bangin' too, but that's really beside the point. Should you find yourself hesitant to reveal more, remember that vulnerability is one of the most alluring qualities a person can express. When you are at ease with your body, it becomes the most captivating thing in the room. Confidence is the finest form of allure, my dear, and it is something no BBL or filter can replicate.

Failing that, get under the covers, count to three and bare thyself. It's like ripping off a plaster, except with the potential for an orgasm shortly afterwards.

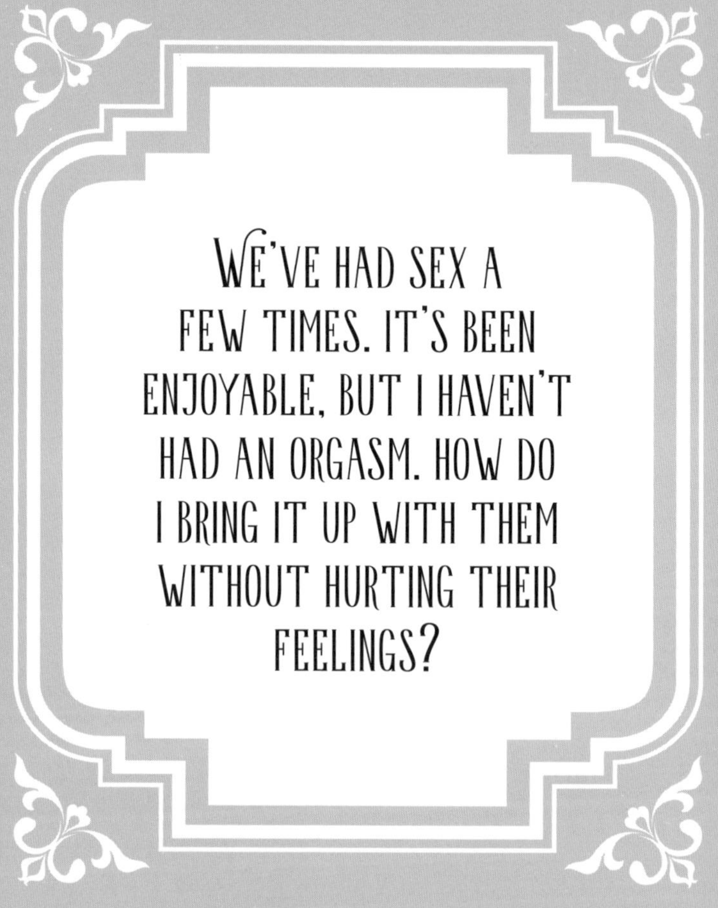

WE'VE HAD SEX A FEW TIMES. IT'S BEEN ENJOYABLE, BUT I HAVEN'T HAD AN ORGASM. HOW DO I BRING IT UP WITH THEM WITHOUT HURTING THEIR FEELINGS?

Dear thoughtful reader,

How charming that in this moment of frustration, your heart reaches out to protect your partner's feelings first.

If you're already au fait with the big 'o' in other contexts, you'll be equipped with the knowledge of what helps you erupt with pleasure. Whether it's having your thingamabobs touched in a certain way, canoodling in a particular position or a kink that makes you feel oh, so good. Do not feel embarrassed to share these titbits with your partner. You are entitled to experience pleasure as much as they already are, and to withhold such a truth from them is to do a disservice to both of you. It also affords the opportunity for them to tell you that they're really into spanking.

Find a quiet moment, when the mood is calm and relaxed, and gently share your thoughts. Approach it with kindness, for the pursuit of mutual satisfaction should be a shared goal. With practice, you should unlock the key to a more fulfilling connection, one hump at a time.

Let's pretend to be really common and wear sneakers and vests!

They want to incorporate roleplay into our sex life, but I'm not sure I'm good at it. How do I get into character without feeling silly?

Dear stage-shy reader,

There is nothing quite like the delightful art of becoming someone else for a spell! While it can feel incredibly silly at first, take heed. It is a vibrant form of play and exploration, no different from other erotic behaviours (except with the occasional need for a costume). And are we not all playing roles of some kind in our daily lives – the dutiful offspring, the enthusiastic employee? Is the erotically charged sailor really such a stretch?

Think of it as a masquerade ball, where you slip into a character, lose yourself, and get swept up in the moment. However, if the prospect of metamorphosis seems daunting, start small. Choose a simple scenario that you both find intriguing (nurse and patient, homemaker and plumber, or simply two strangers meeting at a bar) to ease into the experience.

Remember, you are not treading the boards in London's West End – no one is expecting a Shakespearean performance. Embrace the joviality of the game and bid your self-consciousness adieu. A laugh here, a playful gesture there and before you know it, your gladiator costume will be in the corner of the bedroom while you cry out in pleasure, no acting required.

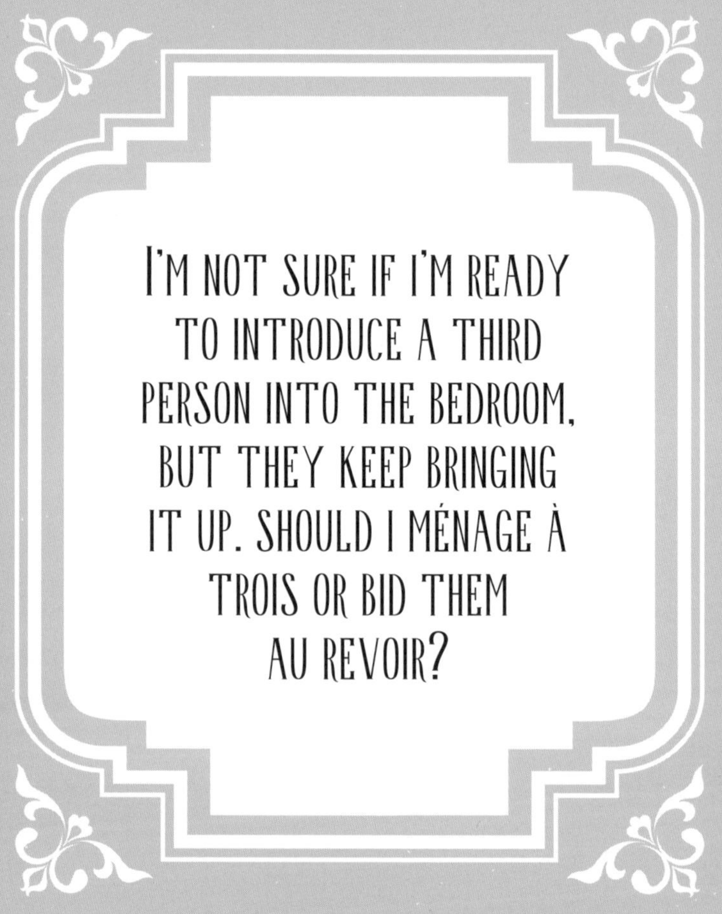
I'M NOT SURE IF I'M READY
TO INTRODUCE A THIRD
PERSON INTO THE BEDROOM,
BUT THEY KEEP BRINGING
IT UP. SHOULD I MÉNAGE À
TROIS OR BID THEM
AU REVOIR?

Dear cautious reader,

Mathematics may not be my strongest suit, devoid as it is of passion and penises, but this is a numbers problem I'm determined to help you solve.

Is this a sexual escapade that will bring your hearts closer or are they seeking a pathway to permanent polyamory? If the former prevails, consider the positives – perhaps their regard for you is so rampant and their affections so secure, they feel comfortable to share your most intimate moments with a third party. The titillation is for you both to enjoy – the stars of your love story – not the sexy stranger who may make a guest appearance. Your discomfort might be assuaged by the pleasure on offer – but it's really your choice to make.

If a lifestyle change is more attuned with their ultimate desire, this decision bears more weight. Do you want to keep them (and their sexy bum) all to yourself or are you willing to share? This might mean finding yourself part of a throuple, foursome, or left out in the cold on occasion while they engage in a little ménage à deux without you.

I haven't washed my bits in two weeks!
I love it when you talk dirty, darling.

They've suggested talking dirty during sex, but I'm too shy. How do I ease into it without feeling embarrassed?

Dear tongue-tied reader,

We cannot all be blessed with a wicked tongue that can tease and tantalize at a moment's notice. But that shouldn't deter you from throwing caution to the wind and using yours all the same.

Engaging in passionate parlance need not be a shameful spectacle. It's something one can ease into, a playful exploration of the realms of desire (and a whole lot of fun). To get started, why not begin your dirty diatribe by penning messages to your lover. Or perhaps a conversation via telephone to keep your blushes at bay.

In person, if your partner is particularly keen, ask them to begin. Let them set the tone for how dirty we're talking here. Perhaps their preferred language errs on the side of Mills & Boon rather than hard-core pornographic. Testing the waters with your words and seeing how they react verbally and physically will give you a good indication that you're hitting the sweet spot.

I HAVE A HAIRY BUSH, BUT MY PARTNER WOULD PREFER THAT I DIDN'T. SHOULD I CHANGE MY GROOMING HABITS TO KEEP THEM HAPPY?

Dear furry reader,

They say the course of true love never runs smooth, but that doesn't mean your skin has to. A gentleperson's particular persuasion, when it comes to their tresses (above the neck and below), is theirs alone, and don't let anyone try to convince or comb you otherwise.

If you love your pubic patch and have no intention of a hedge trim, let your partner know your foliage is staying put. If they can't see the wood for the trees or get accustomed to your unique topiary, that's on them.

That said, it's a stark reality that hair doth grow back. Perhaps you've taken a laissez-faire approach to personal grooming of late and wouldn't object to switching things up. If you are ready, willing and have the necessary equipment/beautician standing by, you might consider laying it all bare for a month or two for their pleasure and your own curiosity. Perhaps you'll feel friskier without your usual barnet? And what's the worst that can happen? You'll feel the winter chill a little more keenly and be back to your furry self in a few weeks.

Lovely bush
Could do with a trim

'All the privilege I claim for my own sex (it is not a very enviable one: you need not covet it), is that of loving longest, when existence or when hope is gone!'

Persuasion, Jane Austen

Lady Bennet-Down's Tips

- ## SERVE PASSION WITH A SIDE OF DISCRETION

  Some thrills are worth the wait, especially if it means keeping your Uber rating intact.

- ## THE BEST PERFORMANCE IN BED ISN'T AN ACT

  Curiosity, communication and a willingness to laugh are far more seductive than perfection.

- ## CONFIDENCE IS THE BEST BEDROOM ATTIRE

  No filter or influencer physique can outshine someone at ease in their own skin.

- ## ROLEPLAY IS A MASQUERADE MADE FOR TWO

  Lean into the silliness, let go of self-consciousness and remember, there isn't an Olivier award on the line.

- ## THREE'S COMPANY, BUT ONLY IF EVERYONE'S ON BOARD

  Consent and comfort are the foundation of any ménage à trois (and a solid bed frame).

- ## CLEAN UP WITH DIRTY TALK

  Start small, stay playful, and remember it's supposed to be fun, not flawless.

VII

The Greatest Showmance

'Every distinguishing attention that could be paid, was paid to her. To amuse her, and be agreeable in her eyes, seemed all that he cared for.'

Emma, Jane Austen

YOUR HEART'S ALL A FLUTTER AND YOU'RE BEING ROYALLY RIDDEN ON A REGULAR BASIS. YES, DEAR READER, YOU ARE WELL AND TRULY IN RELATIONSHIP TERRITORY.

STEPPING OUT IN SOCIETY AS A BONA FIDE COUPLE WILL HAVE YOU ASKING HOW SOON IS TOO SOON TO TELL THE WORLD YOU'RE ROMANTICALLY ENTANGLED? WHAT PUBLIC BEHAVIOUR RUNS THE RISK OF GIVING YOU THE ICK? AND HOW DO YOU DEAL WITH JEALOUS EXES REARING THEIR RATHER ATTRACTIVE HEADS? WHATEVER CONCERNS YOU DO ENCOUNTER, TRY TO ENJOY YOUR NEW-FOUND COUPLE STATUS, DON'T OVERTHINK EVERY POST AND LIKE AND TAKE IT ONE SOCIALLY AWARE STEP AT A TIME.

NEW COUPLE ALERT

THEY WANT TO FILM A TIKTOK OF US DOING A CRINGEY COUPLE'S DANCE, BUT I'M NOT SURE IT'S MY THING. HOW DO I LET THEM DOWN WITHOUT PUSHING THEM AWAY?

Dear socially awkward reader,

True love takes many forms. Presently, one of those is sharing the art of coordinated dancing to popular music. It declares to the world: 'We are a couple and we're so in love we took the time to rehearse and make this video to show you how perfect our lives are. Also, we are good at dancing. And look how nice our kitchen is.'

I understand why this might not be a statement you're ready to make, now or ever. Whether you're a truly terrible dancer, an influencer with an impeccable TikTok presence you need to protect or a socially elusive caterpillar unwilling to break out of your cocoon (or break out those dance moves) - open your heart and share your concerns. Make sure your dance-crazed darling knows your dissent is based on your social preferences, not your feelings towards them.

Of course, you could just give it a go. Successful relationships require compromise, so this might be the practice you need.

They just posted a selfie of us on Instagram, but we haven't talked about going public. How soon is too soon to be Insta-official?

Dear selfie-conscious reader,

The alarm of being outed before you're ready is very real. Perchance you have other suitors you would like to inform of your attachment first or a pushy parent that believes sexual entanglements before marriage are sinful. Giving one another forewarning when you're thinking of going public is just common courtesy, even if your new beau thinks they're just being cute.

That said, if you have no objection to revelling in your new romance, there is no 'too soon' when it comes to regaling the world, virtually or otherwise. As long as the feelings are mutual, make the most of this honeymoon period. Shower your followers with rainbows, hearts, butterflies – the lot.

But be warned, heavy is the head that wears the 'I've just been dumped' baseball hat over unwashed hair. A fall from the loved-up loft can be particularly painful. So, if you err on the side of caution, pare back your PDA and spare the world from endless selfies until the relationship has had the time to take root.

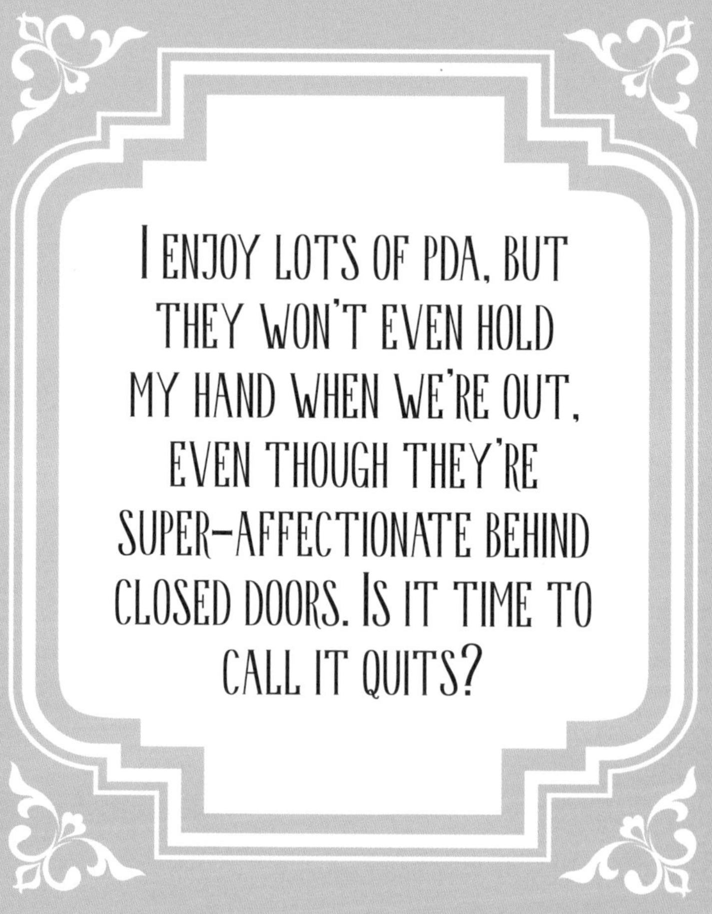
I ENJOY LOTS OF PDA, BUT THEY WON'T EVEN HOLD MY HAND WHEN WE'RE OUT, EVEN THOUGH THEY'RE SUPER-AFFECTIONATE BEHIND CLOSED DOORS. IS IT TIME TO CALL IT QUITS?

Dear touchy-feely reader,

Public displays of affection were once considered the height of impropriety. While not quite de rigueur, nowadays holding hands, embracing and kissing beyond the confines of your own bed chamber are acceptable and, in many cases, socially encouraged.

To openly and demonstratively exhibit your love comes naturally to some, yourself included, and I can see why. It conveys your private thoughts of attraction, desire and intimacy at those times when it's just not the done thing to strip off and pounce on your partner (at the library, in a restaurant, in their parents' kitchen, et cetera). It also helps to define your relationship and reassure the other person that they aren't just another friend.

But for your private paramour, that is not the case. They might feel all the same things you do but prefer to express them when you are away from prying eyes. It's important to respect this while trying to meet each other halfway. Broach the subject and see where they might be willing to expand their habitual horizons. Holding hands seems like an ideal place to start rather than asking for them to proffer oral copulation at the theatre. If they're uninterested in reaching out, figuratively and literally, a hard decision might be coming your way (just don't expect a hug if you break up).

THEIR EX HAS FOLLOWED ME ONLINE AND HAS LIKED PICTURES OF US TOGETHER. IS SHE JUST BEING KIND OR KINDA CREEPY?

Dear ex-asperated reader,

Embarking down the road of romance with a new lover means knowing you're rarely the only person to have trodden that same path. More often than not, one's previous passions can remain very much in the past (thank goodness). But on occasion they insert themselves into your present and require attention.

Firstly, establish the ex's motives - are they on friendly terms with your partner? Have they clearly moved on? If yes, chances are they're just happy to see their ex living their best life with you. If not, their motives could be murkier, and it might be easier to remove them as a follower before things deteriorate. Engaging your other half in this debate is essential, as they will have greater insight into their ex's true intentions. Proceed with caution, dear reader. Sometimes a 'like' is just a like. Sometimes it's a shit-show waiting in the wings.

'SHE MUST BE USED TO THE CONSIDERATION OF HIS BEING IN LOVE WITH HER, AND THEN A RETURN OF AFFECTION MIGHT NOT BE VERY DISTANT.'

MANSFIELD PARK, JANE AUSTEN

Lady Bennet-Down's Tips

IT'S OFFICIAL: DISCUSS YOUR SOCIAL INTENTIONS

An Instagram debut should feel exciting, not ambushing. Chat about your plans before hitting 'post.'

DANCE CRAZES AREN'T FOR EVERYONE

If a TikTok duet makes you squirm, be honest, stay kind, and maybe offer to hold the camera instead.

ROMANCE DOESN'T THRIVE ON AUTOPILOT

Small gestures, thoughtful questions, and a dash of surprise keep the spark alive.

PUT YOUR PDA NEEDS OUT THERE

Affection comes in many forms, so find a rhythm that works for you both, even if it starts with just holding hands.

WATCH OUT FOR EX-TREME BEHAVIOUR

An ex in your likes isn't always a red flag - communicate with your partner before jumping to conclusions.

BOUNDARIES ARE THE UNSUNG HEROES OF INTIMACY

Set them clearly, respect them fully and remember that comfort creates chemistry.

VIII

The Ghosting

'If I could but know his heart, everything would become easy.'

Sense and Sensibility by Jane Austen

WRAP UP WARM, DEAR READER, BECAUSE IT'S COLD SHOULDER TIME. UNFORTUNATELY, GHOSTING – THAT GHASTLY AFFAIR WHEN YOU SEE NEITHER HIDE NOR HAIR OF YOUR BELOVED – HAS BECOME AN EVERYDAY PART OF DATING. IF YOU FIND YOURSELF IN A SCENARIO WHERE YOUR PARAMOUR HAS BECOME PARANORMAL, FEAR NOT; I HAVE PLENTY OF WISDOM TO SHARE TO HELP YOU NAVIGATE THESE HORRORS (EVEN IF YOU'RE THINKING ABOUT SLIPPING INTO AN INVISIBILITY CLOAK YOURSELF).

THEY STOPPED REPLYING TO MY MESSAGES, BUT I CAN SEE THEY'RE STILL WATCHING MY STORIES. SHOULD I CONFRONT THEM OR JUST LET IT GO?

Dear haunted reader,

It sounds like you may have an indecisive apparition on your hands. A spirit lingering in limbo, unsure of whether to be gone from your life while looming large, making their presence known. As spooky as it may seem, this behaviour is in the realm of normality and is no great cause for alarm ... yet.

For someone with so little regard for your feelings, it seems superfluous to waste any more of your energy on them. A confrontation will only stoke your resentment of their reticence and leave you all a fluster. Their social movements, however subtle, are a clear sign they have not dropped down dead. While they might still enjoy a snoop, if they're not invested enough to actually return your attentions, it's time to cut them off. How dare they enjoy the spoils of your inner circle if they're determined to stay out of sight.

If blocking them feels too severe, have your wits about you. The longer they linger, the more pronounced your heart ache may become. And the more forgiving you might feel if they slide into your DMs. Make no mistake - you've seen a ghost and a second haunting is highly likely.

You vex me
NO NEW MESSAGES

I've developed the ick and am no longer interested. Is it ever okay to ghost or do I owe them an explanation?

Dear ghoulish reader,

I thought your skin was looking a little translucent. It would appear the call of the underworld is strong and you, yourself, are planning to disappear into thin air. However, before you slip into something white and floaty, good manners (of which I'm sure you possess many) would dictate that a brief explanation is warranted.

You have delighted this person with your company, dined and danced with them, maybe even invited them into your bed chamber. If you're as spectacular as they say, there's a chance your sudden absence will hurt and confuse them, which I'm sure the gentleperson within you would prefer to avoid. There's also the chance their feelings are mutual. Bringing the issue to a close alleviates them of having to say anything too.

If, however, you take the trouble to explain your feelings and curtail the attachment, and they continue to pursue you, a ghosting is not out of the question. Joining the spirit world (metaphorically, of course) might be the only way to send a clear message and prevent further persistence.

THEY GHOSTED ME, BUT I KEEP BUMPING INTO THEM AT OUR USUAL SPOTS. HOW DO I HANDLE IT?

Dear startled reader,

Once a haunting has begun, its subject can quickly become comfortable with the new status quo. No doubt the hole in your heart is toiling to mend itself while your mind struggles to make sense of being so boldly ignored. So I can only imagine the distress these regular spectral sightings are having on you. Being thrust into the presence of the dead while you're picking up your vanilla latte or sweating out a set of dead lifts is unnerving to say the least.

Please know that short of packing your trunk chest and catching a wagon out of town, there is no easy fix here. But there are two courses of action to consider. Firstly, you could feign ignorance, turn up your podcast and blank them back. Do not feel ashamed to save face and swan around like their muteness means nothing to you.

Secondly, you could be the bigger person, which is something that never feels as good as it sounds. Stride over and greet them with grace. Avoid any hint of flirtation and keep to neutral topics, like work or the weather. They might feel sheepish and attempt to explain their behaviour, but the ghostly elephant in the room will remain. Please know, your actions are unlikely to sway them to relinquish their silence. So, the choice, my dear, is yours.

'I CAN LISTEN NO LONGER IN SILENCE. I MUST SPEAK TO YOU BY SUCH MEANS AS ARE WITHIN MY REACH. YOU PIERCE MY SOUL. I AM HALF AGONY, HALF HOPE. TELL ME NOT THAT I AM TOO LATE, THAT SUCH PRECIOUS FEELINGS ARE GONE FOREVER.'

PERSUASION, JANE AUSTEN

Lady Bennet-Down's Tips

- ## VANISHING ACTS RARELY WIN ENCORES

If you're tempted to ghost, remember that honesty (however brief) is often kinder than silence.

- ## THE SECRET'S OUT: THEY'RE A STALKER

If someone ghosts you but keeps lurking, their subtle hints and bizarre intent isn't yours to decode.

- ## DON'T WASTE TIME ON SECOND CHANCES

One unanswered text might be an oversight, three are a sign. Put your phone away and preserve your dignity.

- ## THEY'RE JUST NOT THAT INTO YOU

While a kidnapping or infectious disease are possible, they're far from probable. Stop seeking answers and start moving on.

- ## SILENCE IS DEAFENING BUT TRY TO HEAR IT

If they want to talk, they'll reach out. In the meantime, you've got a life to live.

- ## YOU'RE NOT A REVOLVING DOOR

If someone disappears and reappears as if nothing happened, don't be afraid to set boundaries or build massive walls.

IX

The Split

'I BELIEVE IN A TRUE ANALOGY BETWEEN OUR BODILY FRAMES AND OUR MENTAL; AND THAT AS OUR BODIES ARE THE STRONGEST, SO ARE OUR FEELINGS; CAPABLE OF BEARING MOST ROUGH USAGE, AND RIDING OUT THE HEAVIEST WEATHER.'

***PERSUASION*, JANE AUSTEN**

WOE IS YOU. WOE IS THEM. WOE IS THE ROTTEN APPLE THAT IS THIS UNGODLY SITUATION. A BREAK-UP IS THE VERY ANTIPATHY OF MERRIMENT, THE AVERSION TO FELICITY, THE RUINER OF RAPTURE. THIS HOLDS TRUE WHETHER YOU'RE THE HOODED GHOUL BEHIND THE GUILLOTINE OR THE DISMEMBERED, YOUR HEAD LOLLING IN A BLOODIED BASKET. BECAUSE BREAK-UPS ARE HARD FOR EVERYONE EVEN WHEN YOU KNOW THEY'RE FOR THE BEST.

TIME IS THE GREATEST HEALER (AND A LITTLE SEXY REBOUND WOULDN'T GO AMISS). OTHER THAN WATCHING THE CLOCK, HERE'S A LITTLE WISDOM TO GUIDE YOU THROUGH THIS DARKEST OF TUNNELS. A FEW SMALL GLIMMERS OF LIGHT THAT WILL HOPEFULLY AMELIORATE THE AWFULNESS AND GET YOU OUT THE OTHER SIDE IN ONE PIECE WITH YOUR DIGNITY STILL INTACT.

We said we'd stay friends, but seeing their posts with someone new feels like a knife to the heart. Should I unfollow their socials or just suffer in silence?

Dear wounded reader,

As a new love emerges like spring flowers blossoming on their socials, so heartache truly takes root in your soul. What a pain to endure! We humans are masochistic beings, of that, I am sure. As we wither and wilt under the strain of lost love, so do we seek out the one thing that will wound us further – a shiny selfie of our former beloved entwined and enraptured with another.

While enduring a hushed agony may seem noble, I am here to tell you it is a fool's errand. There is nothing to be gained from doom-scrolling, 'doom' being the operative word here. You may have vowed to stay friends, but for now aloofness is the order of the day. Mute or unfollow their socials, cutting yourself off at the source. This will give you the room you need to self-nurture, repair and replenish your own cup, one cat video at a time.

Only then, when your own petals have unfurled and turned towards the sun and your heart has healed, can you begin to consider checking in on past lives (and snooping on their new partner who is undoubtedly inferior to you).

They have my favourite hoodie, but asking for it back feels petty. Should I let it go or stage a retrieval mission?

Dear hoodless reader,

When heartbreak descends, it takes no prisoners, except, of course, if you've been careless enough to leave personal affects at the residence of your former flame. From corsets and greatcoats to pantaloons and pelisses, your home and theirs are likely littered with remnants of this recent affair.

But just because love is lost, it doesn't mean your favourite garments need to be. While I must protest against the notion of a secret rescue mission (your hoodie is not worth the humiliation if you get caught), perhaps a trade is in order? Do you have something of theirs they might be missing just as much – a band tee, a pricey perfume or a sex toy that you're definitely not planning on using alone?

With no bad blood between you, there's little reason a rendezvous cannot be set to make a swift exchange. Keep the meeting brief and courteous so you don't poke still-healing wounds. But if you have nothing of theirs to offer but a rusty razor or empty deodorant bottle, it might be time to bid your hoodie adieu. Consider it something for them to remember you by and treat yourself to a new one.

WE SHARE A FRIENDSHIP GROUP, AND NOW EVERY SOCIAL EVENT FEELS LIKE A MINEFIELD. DO I STAY HOME OR SUCK IT UP?

Dear explosive reader,

When lives become entangled in love, so too do acquaintances. Sometimes true, lasting friendships can be found in the world of another, and it feels too painful to give them up when so much has been forfeited already. And sometimes you simply desire the freedom to enter a ballroom safe in the knowledge chandeliers will not shatter (oh the drama!).

We all need our nearest and dearest to guide us through the difficulty of a break-up, so be considerate. If these friends were originally your partner's, perhaps wait until the dust has settled - you can always engage individuals one on one to ensure friendships are not lost. Likewise, if they were yours, I'd expect your partner to follow suit.

For friends that fall into mutual territory, inform the host you're planning to attend an event so they can convey the facts to your ex. If you both show up somewhere unexpectedly, be kind, keep your distance, but remember you have a right to be there. Chances are, once the first ball has been overcome, you'll feel fine to dance the night away at any soiree where they might wander in.

I was the one who ended things, but now I'm regretting it. Do I reach out or is that just reopening old wounds?

Dear regretful reader,

Should, would, could are all words best left out of our vocabularies, because regrets never leave us. They fester and eat away at our insides, taunting us as we try, fruitlessly, to move on with our lives. In direct response, yes, my dear, to reach out to your beloved will undoubtedly be tugging at their stitches, setting them back in efforts to put you out of sight, out of mind.

But does that mean it is wrong? Only you know how far you pushed them, how wounded their heart was, how likely they are to reconsider and reconcile. If the choice was yours, there must have been good reason. What has caused this sea change? Is it a fear of loneliness, facing the hellscape that is the modern world of dating, or the thought of them lying with another that troubles you so?

Before you act hastily, revisit your former decision, perhaps seeking counsel from close acquaintances familiar with the relationship's tides and turns. This should provide perspective and help ascertain whether reunification is right for your romantic future. If you're resolute, then I wish you all the best. May they feel as you do, may their heart be open and may their wounds heal with no scars.

'A man does not recover from such a devotion of the heart to such a woman! He ought not; he does not.'

Persuasion, Jane Austen

Lady Bennet-Down's Tips

MUTUAL FRIENDS REQUIRE MUTUAL GRACE

Tread carefully, communicate openly, and remember, shared spaces are no place for dramatic duels or daggered glares.

SOCIAL MEDIA SILENCE IS GOLDEN

If their posts feel like poison, mute, unfollow and reclaim your peace. Doom-scrolling will never serve your broken heart.

WHAT'S YOURS MIGHT NOW BE THEIRS

Some personal items are worth retrieving from your ex, while others are worth letting go (your copy of *Fifty Shades of Grey*). Know the difference.

REGRET IS A FICKLE MISTRESS

Before reopening old wounds, be certain it's love you're seeking, not just fear of whatever comes next (including Tinder).

WORDS UNSENT CAN STILL HEAL

A love letter needn't find its recipient to serve its purpose. Burn it along with some marshmallows or keep it to remember the good times.

TIME HEALS, BUT TACT HELPS

Whether you're leaving quietly or lingering briefly, kindness is the greatest parting gift.

X

The Glow-up

'She had some feelings which she was ashamed to investigate. They were too much like joy, senseless joy!'

***Persuasion*, Jane Austen**

How wonderful it is to be footloose and fancy free, and looking to the horizon filled with hope and happiness. Congratulations, my dear, you've made it through to the other side and you're ready to shine #blessed.

Of course, glowing up is a little like growing up – there are still hurdles to overcome along the way. Luckily, my wisdom is here to guide you, so you can get on with looking fine, feeling finer and enjoying the finest things life has to offer.

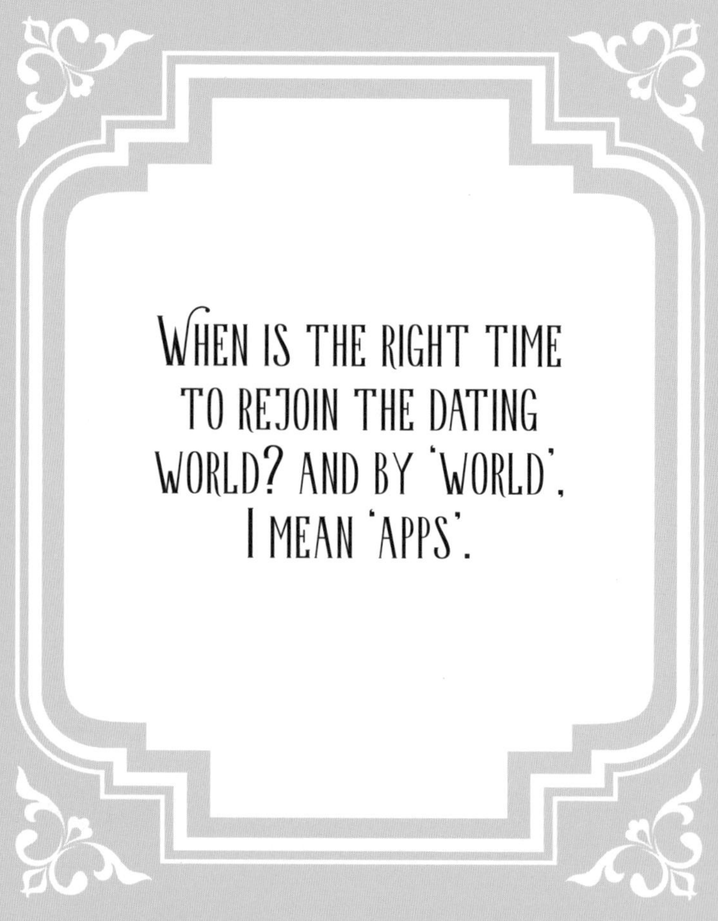

When is the right time to rejoin the dating world? And by 'world', I mean 'apps'.

Dear eager reader,

It occurs to me, if you've already considered tweaking that profile and getting back on the virtual dating horse, then singledom has descended and you are in its throes. But there's no urgency to swipe, no need to force new connections, so if you feel pressured by society or uninterested in making a new love-match, hold firm. The time to return will make itself known and the apps will still be there in all their detrital glory.

For truly there is no perfect moment to dive once again into the fray, to brace for the inevitable highs and lows, goings and comings (hopefully more of the latter) of modern dating. If you've been out of the pool for some time, it might feel scary, awkward or even titillating to dip your toes in. My advice? Feel all those feelings and take it one swipe at a time.

Oh, and cherish it while it lasts, because soon enough you will find yourself bewitched and betrothed yet again, bound to another by love and IKEA furniture.

I BUMPED INTO MY EX WHEN I WAS LOOKING LIKE A VISION, BUT THEY WEREN'T DOING SO GREAT. SHOULD I SAY SOMETHING OR SIMPLY SASHAY AWAY?

Dear radiant reader,

Some loves leave a bitter taste in our mouths (or worse), whilst others we can look back on with deep affection – a congenial chapter in our romantic tale. However honourable we consider ourselves to be, when fate throws us into the path of the former, we may take pleasure in their demise or despair, for it feels just that they should suffer for past wrongs.

But when we're being our most admirable or when it is the latter we encounter in the cereal aisle, it can be painful to see our former loves forlorn. Even more so when we're so clearly thriving. But walking away without saying a word would be a wasted opportunity to exhibit true grace.

Perhaps, dear reader, it's worth bearing in mind your less visionary moments in the quiet of home, when you have a wobble and eat a block of cheddar. Extending this less-than-perfect reality to your ex with a self-deprecating comment or show of solidarity could help lift their spirits – at the very least they won't feel even worse about themselves than before they bumped into you.

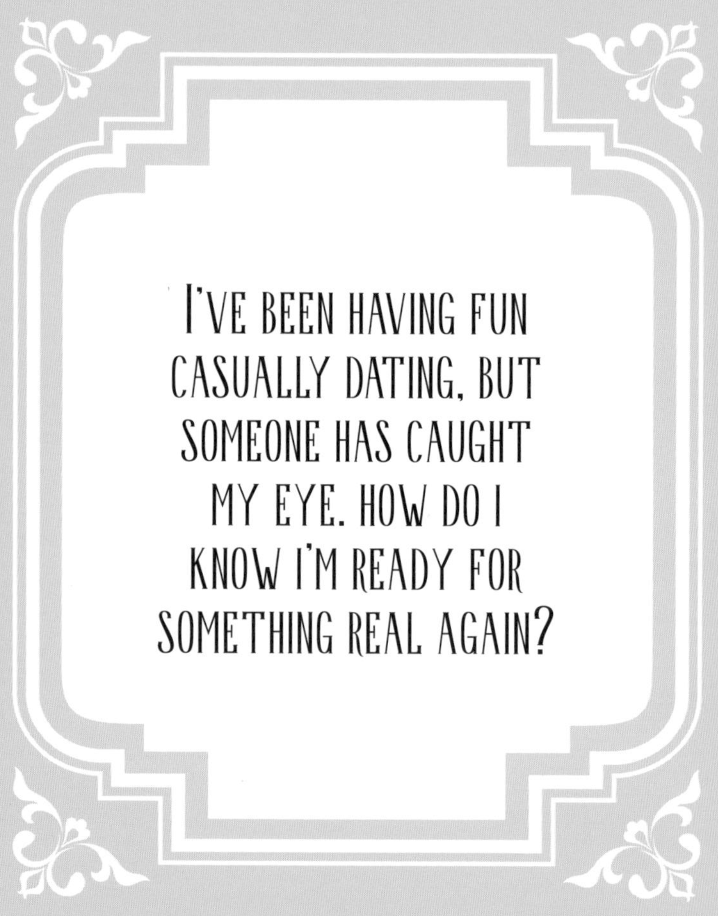

I'VE BEEN HAVING FUN CASUALLY DATING, BUT SOMEONE HAS CAUGHT MY EYE. HOW DO I KNOW I'M READY FOR SOMETHING REAL AGAIN?

Dear cautious reader,

Zooks! Is it time to clamber aboard the merry-go-round of love already? Unfortunately, Cupid does not care for the clock. That pesky cherub can strike arrows at a moment's notice, plunging you into love's warm glow without warning.

Oftentimes, when you know, you really do know. Sparks fly, butterflies flutter, and the room parts like the sea drawing you to them. But for injured parties, still reeling for their previous turn, it can feel too soon to succumb once again to the ride. Better to continue to fill one's dance card with an array of frivolous fancies than get caught up in the heart of a single suitor before you're ready.

If you can't bear to see then slip through the net, a healthy compromise might be to share your concerns – let this sweetheart know your heart if still healing. And remember not to rush. Love has no finish line. If they're truly worthy, they'll be willing to wait.

MY GLOW-UP IS COMPLETE, BUT I FEEL PRESSURE TO 'WIN' THE BREAK-UP. HOW DO I FOCUS ON MY HAPPINESS NOT THEIRS?

Dear competitive reader,

When the dust on a dalliance has settled, everyone wants to know they're doing far better than their former flame. The road to recovery can feel like a racetrack – your ex-partner positioned beside you as you hurtle towards some imaginary demarcation of 'completely fine'.

It might be tantalizing to flaunt your glow-up around town, gossip about them with mutual acquaintances, and post pleasing self-portraits to hammer the point home on your socials. But that would be bad form, dear one. You say your glow-up is complete, but your competitive streak signals that you still have a little healing to attend to. Rather than look outwards, constantly comparing how well you're doing, your time would be better spent on inner reflection.

Take the waters in Bath (or just in your bath), work on your mental health, spend time with your friends. These curative activities will bring you back to yourself and help you find true resolution. By then, you won't care an iota what your ex is up to. You'll be glowing too damn much. Pardon my French.

‘Next to being married, a girl likes to be crossed in love a little now and then. It is something to think of, and gives her a sort of distinction among her companions.’

Pride and Prejudice, Jane Austen

Lady Bennet-Down's Tips

YOU'LL KNOW WHEN YOU'RE READY

Whether it's dating apps or blind dates, trust your gut before you dive back into the dating pool.

GLOWING UP IS NOT LINEAR

The odd bad day is to be expected. You can fake it till you make it, but it's also ok to not be ok. Let people in and share your struggles.

HOW YOU DOIN'?

If you cross paths with an amiable ex, don't gloat at their downfall. Be grateful you're glowing and say something to help them get their shine back.

TAKE CARE WHEN SLIPPING INTO SOMETHING MORE SERIOUS

Ready to saddle up or feeling uncertain? Honesty with yourself and your new suitor is the surest path forward.

CONFIDENCE IS CUTEST WHEN IT'S JUST FOR YOU

Post those selfies because you want to, not because your ex might be snooping.

GLOWING-UP IS A FEELING, NOT A FINISH LINE

Celebrate your milestones, but remember, getting back to happiness isn't a competition (even with yourself).

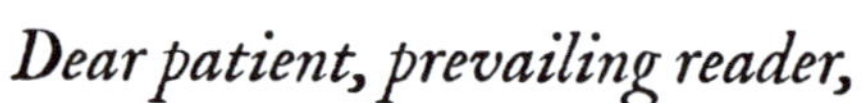

Dear patient, prevailing reader,

When I set quill to parchment, my goal was to imbue you with the wisdom I've gleaned navigating romantic tribulations and titillations amongst the Ton. I wanted these words to fortify your spirit as you step out in society and revel in its revelries – from ballroom etiquette and dining decorum to going public and boudoir behaviours.

I do hope my counsel has been a guiding light, especially through the most vexing of moments – those inexplicable ghostings and agonizing break-ups – that seem to have taken a reprehensible foothold in modern dating rituals.

Now, I must take my leave, for there is wine to drink, dancefloors to grace and merriment to be made ...

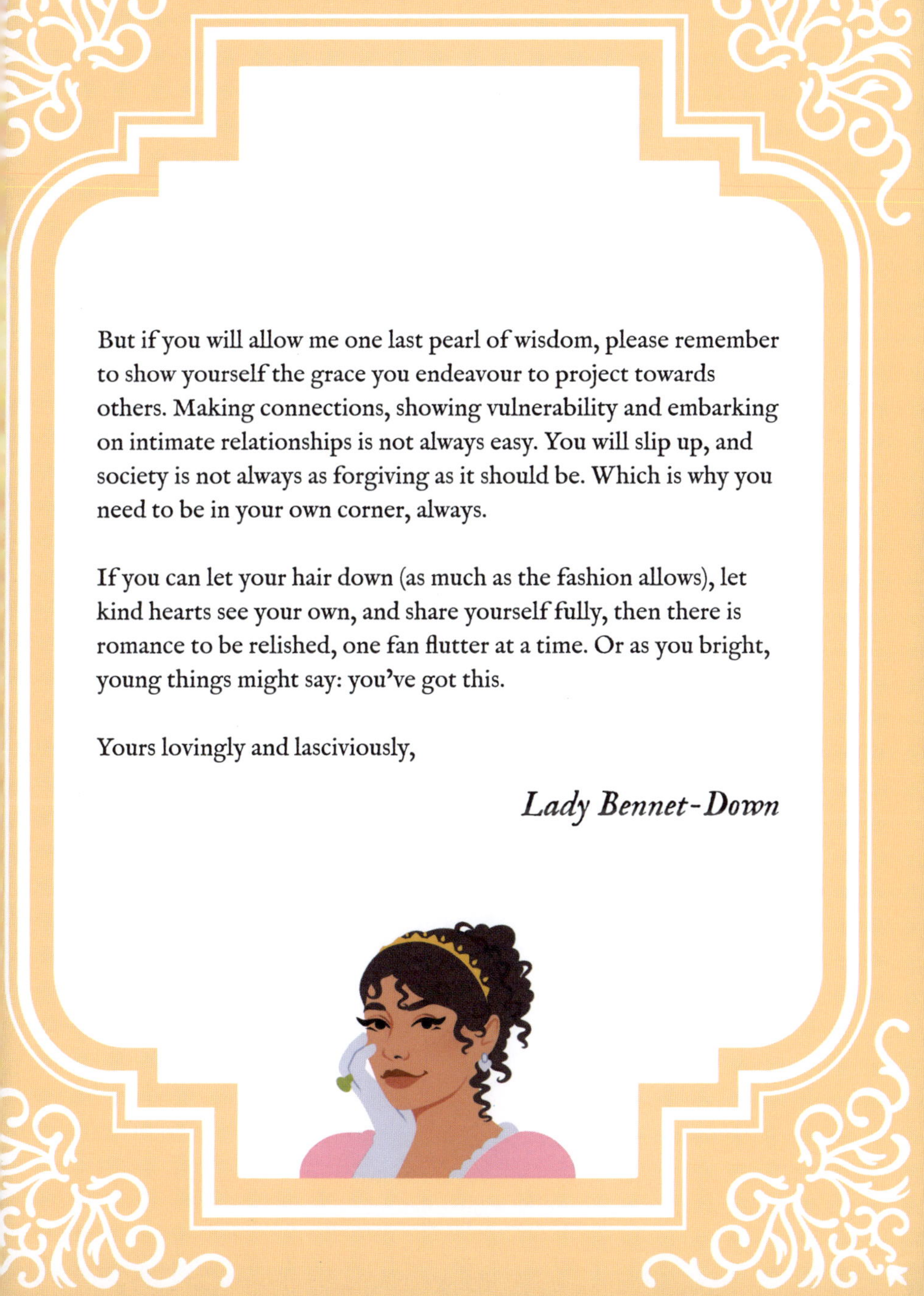

But if you will allow me one last pearl of wisdom, please remember to show yourself the grace you endeavour to project towards others. Making connections, showing vulnerability and embarking on intimate relationships is not always easy. You will slip up, and society is not always as forgiving as it should be. Which is why you need to be in your own corner, always.

If you can let your hair down (as much as the fashion allows), let kind hearts see your own, and share yourself fully, then there is romance to be relished, one fan flutter at a time. Or as you bright, young things might say: you've got this.

Yours lovingly and lasciviously,

Lady Bennet-Down